Teenage Parents

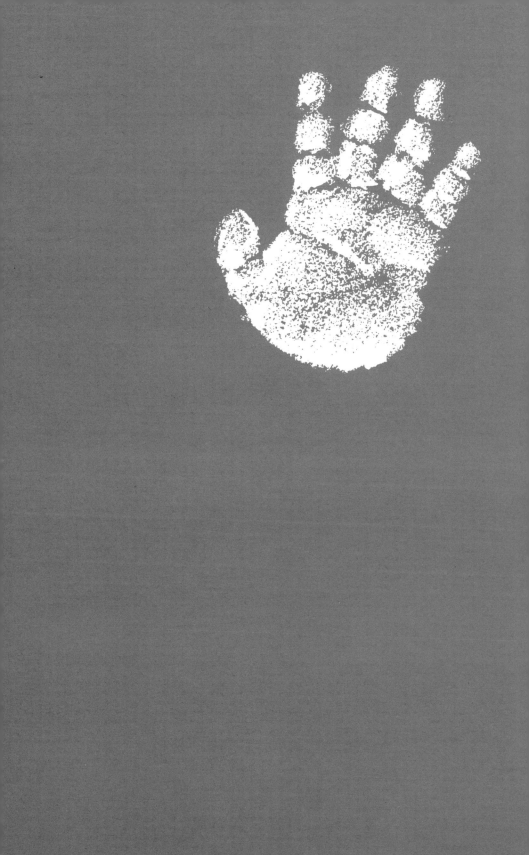

TEENAGE PARENTS

by
John Glore

The Rourke Corporation, Inc.

For Julie and Alexa

The Rourke Corporation, Inc.
P.O. Box 3328, Vero Beach, FL 32964

Glore, John, 1955-
    Teenage parents / by John Glore
        p. cm. — (The Family)
    Includes bibliographical references (p. 62-63) and index.
    Summary: Discusses teenage pregnancy, its problems, and alternative choices and
methods of dealing with the situation.
    ISBN 0-86593-080-5
    1. Teenage mothers—United States—Juvenile literature.
 ✓2. Teenage pregnancy—United States—Juvenile literature.
    [1. Pregnancy. 2. Teenage parents.] I. Title II. Series: Family
(Vero Beach, Fla.)
HQ759.4.G58 1990
362.83'92—dc20
                                                                                      90-8758
                                                                                          CIP
                                                                                           AC

Series Editor: Gregory Lee
Editors: Elizabeth Sirimarco, Marguerite Aronowitz
Book design and production: The Creative Spark,
    Capistrano Beach, CA
Cover illustration: Rob Court

Teenage Parents

Contents

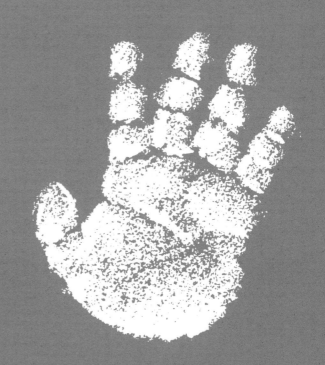

I. A Growing Problem

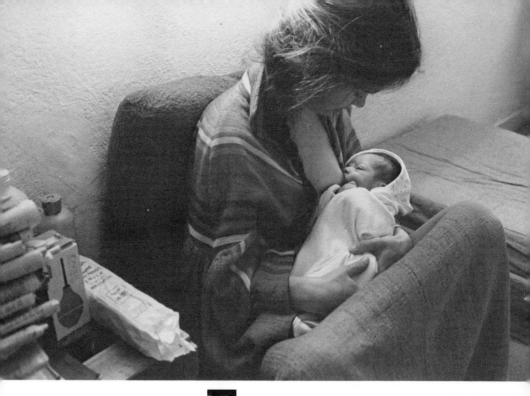

Every year, over one million teenage girls in the United States become pregnant.

Chances are you have picked up this book for one of two reasons. The first is that you yourself are one of those million. You are either a pregnant teenager, or you're worried that you might be. A few months ago you probably never dreamed this could happen to you. Sometimes you still feel like a kid yourself, and now you suddenly have to face the possibility of having a child of your own. But from the day you began having sexual relations you became an adult in at least one important way. Now you have some very difficult, adult choices to make.

On the other hand, you may have picked up this book only because you want to know more. Maybe you need to do a report for school, or maybe you have a friend who is pregnant and you want to be able to help her. Or maybe you're smart

Teenagers who choose to raise their babies must be prepared for the 24-hour care they need. Staying in school and/or keeping a job are large responsibilities when you're a single parent raising a child.

enough to realize that sooner or later you will need to know how to make the right choices for your own life.

Whether your interest is personal or not, you should find this book interesting and useful. You will read about teenage pregnancy in the United States: how common it is, and what effect it has on our society. You will also read about the choices involved for a young woman who is sexually active: choices before, during and after a pregnancy. They are some of the most important choices she will make in her entire life.

The Numbers

The high rate of teenage pregnancy in the United States is a serious problem for our country. While Ronald Reagan was president he set up a special task force just to deal with this growing problem.

Pregnancy happens to teenage girls from all walks of life. Many of them are poor, but many come from families who are financially secure. Some don't know much about sex, but some know a great deal. Some are careless, some are careful but unlucky, and many are just not careful enough. In most cases, teenagers become pregnant by accident, but many teenagers choose to become pregnant. They think of it as an escape from problems in their family. Or the idea of having a child is romantic to them. They may also be in a hurry to become adults. Whatever kind of background they come from, and whatever the reasons for their pregnancy, these young women are all part of a large problem for society.

How serious is the problem? You've already read that over one million American teenagers become pregnant each year. That's about 125 girls every hour of every day of the year, or two every minute.

Here's an even more startling number.

Studies predict that four out of every ten young women in the United States will become pregnant before they turn twenty. The United States has the highest rate of teen pregnancy of any major country in the world. More than half of the teenagers who become pregnant will actually give birth.

You might wonder why this high rate of pregnancy and parenthood among teens is a problem, or why it's our problem. After all, if a girl gets pregnant, that's her problem, right? Not quite. Teenage pregnancy and parenthood affect our whole society in many ways.

The Cost

To begin with, most teenagers who become pregnant end up turning to government sources for financial support for themselves and their babies. The government has a number of welfare programs to help, and these programs are paid for by the rest of us through taxes. Teenage pregnancy and parenthood cost the government billions of dollars every year. But money is just one issue.

The cost of teenage pregnancy doesn't end when the baby is born. Most teenage mothers never finish high school, and very few go on to college. Teenage fathers also drop out of school at a high rate. This lowers the overall level of education for our country's young people. The less education a person has, the harder it is to find a good job. So it becomes more likely that he or she will end up turning to the government for support.

Less education in society also means slower progress for our country in general. For example, what if a bright young girl who might have made a great scientific discovery later in her life gets pregnant and decides to drop out of school? She doesn't get the education needed to become a

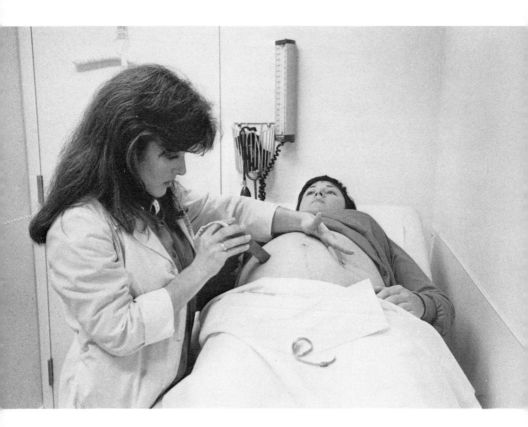

scientist, so she isn't able to make her discovery. What happens when you multiply that one girl times several million? Human progress suffers.

Teen pregnancy generates its own chain reaction, too. Children born to teenage mothers are more likely to be poor all their lives. They are also more likely to drop out of school, need government support, possibly turn to crime, and become teenage parents themselves. This chain reaction isn't easy to stop, and every link in this chain becomes another weak link in society.

Teen Pregnancy And Family Problems

Teenage pregnancy also affects society because it affects the family, which is the building block of society. All but a few of the million girls who get pregnant each year have families who will be affected in various ways by the pregnancy.

When a girl becomes pregnant, she may turn to her existing family—her parents and brothers and sisters—for help, or she may try to start a new family by marrying the baby's father. Either way, her pregnancy puts pressure on the people closest to her.

Even if the pregnant teen gets government aid, her needs will affect the family's budget. Her condition also puts an emotional strain on her family. Her parents may feel pain for what has happened to their daughter, for what she will have to face. They may fear for her health. They may feel uncertain about how to guide her.

They may also feel embarrassed about how their friends and neighbors will react. Those with strong religious or moral beliefs might feel ashamed. Parents may feel guilty and think this wouldn't have happened if they had raised her differently. They may feel their daughter has betrayed them, or ignored what she has been taught. They may worry about how the pregnancy will affect other children in the family. Brothers and sisters of a pregnant teenager often have strong emotional reactions to the change in their family's life.

If the pregnant teen chooses to have an abortion, this can also be a painful decision for the whole family. If she chooses to put her baby up for adoption, that, too, can be hard on the family. Most parents find it difficult to accept that the decision about the pregnancy is out of their hands, that it must be made by their daughter and the child's father. If they try to force their daughter to do what they want, it only generates more stress for everyone. If the daughter chooses to keep her baby and live at home, many more problems will have to be faced.

For all these reasons, parents of a pregnant teenager will probably feel great anxiety. The pressures can sometimes be enough to tear a family apart (on the other hand, the pregnant teen who has a strong, loving family will find in them a great source of support).

The pregnant teenager who decides to make a new family with the baby's father will face a different set of hardships. Chances are the father is still a teenager himself. He may resent having to face the responsibility of marriage and being a parent. He may have to drop out of school to find a job, which means he will probably have trouble earning enough money to support a family. Most teenage parents live in poverty, which adds to the emotional strain. The truth is, most marriages between teenage parents end in early divorce.

Teen Pregnancy And Morality

Many people in our country are concerned about the effect of teenage pregnancy on morality, and the effect of changing morality on teenage pregnancy.

Morality is a set of beliefs about how a person should behave. In the past, most Americans felt that sex before marriage was immoral (or bad). This strong moral belief, shared by one's neighbors and passed on from parents to children, meant that fewer teenagers explored sex. As a result, fewer unwed young women became pregnant. More recently, for many reasons, our society's morals concerning sex have changed. Most adults still believe that sex for teenagers isn't a good idea because of the risks involved. They may also feel that most young people aren't mature enough to handle the confusing feelings that come with sex. But not as many people feel sex before marriage is immoral. More and more young people now try sex at a younger age. This is one reason for the high number of teenage pregnancies.

Some people feel that society should return to stricter morals, and state that sex before marriage isn't just a bad idea—it's wrong. They feel that changes in our moral values are "weakening" the country, and the high rate of teen pregnancy is cited to support their case.

Others think our changing morality isn't the problem—it's that education isn't keeping up with the changes in morality. They argue that young people need to be better informed about sex and its effects. They believe that moral values should be chosen not by society, but by each person according to his or her own conscience.

One thing is certain: teenage pregnancy is a problem with no easy answers. Some believe the government should do more by spending more money to educate the nation's youth about the risks of sexual activity, and giving more help to young mothers and their families. Others believe that stronger moral and religious education is the answer. They feel that spending money on sex education only makes it worse, that educating young people about sex makes them more eager to try it. Some even suggest that giving teenage mothers government money to help pay the costs of pregnancy and parenthood teaches them nothing about responsibility.

Teenage pregnancy is a complicated problem because many of its causes are tied closely to other social problems, including poverty, drug abuse, family strife and flaws in our school system. All this makes finding an answer to the problem of teenage pregnancy that much harder.

Regardless of how large a problem this may be for society, it is a far greater one for each young woman who suddenly finds herself with an unwanted pregnancy.

II. Sexual Choices

Any teenage girl who has had her first menstrual period can become pregnant. Age is not a factor. The typical teenage girl has heard a lot about sex from friends, television, movies and adults in her life who want to make sure she understands what it's all about. Still, it is hard for her to be prepared when sex becomes an issue in her life.

Cindy

Cindy is 14 years old, has started going out with boys and has one special boyfriend. She and he are more than just friends. They enjoy kissing and holding each other close. When they are alone together, they become excited and feel confusing urges.

Cindy has reached a time in her life when she will have to begin making some important choices. If she decides to start having sex, she has taken the first step down a long road paved with many tough choices. Every step she takes will mean having a new choice to make, including what to do if she becomes pregnant. She will have to decide whether or not she is ready to have a baby. If, like most teenagers, Cindy feels she isn't ready for that, then she has more choices to make, such as how to protect herself from an unwanted pregnancy. She needs to know that there are several ways to practice birth control, and that some are better than others.

If she has sex without birth control, or if her method of birth control fails, then sooner or later Cindy will get pregnant—probably sooner. Eight out of ten women who are sexually active and don't use birth control get pregnant within one year. Once pregnancy occurs, choices become harder than ever. Now Cindy must decide whether to have the baby or get an abortion—never an easy decision to make.

A teenage girl with an unplanned pregnancy has several options to consider. How the would-be father feels about the pregnancy is one factor that may influence her choice.

If she decides not to have an abortion, she must choose what will happen to the baby after its birth. Will she keep it and try to raise it, or will she give it up for adoption? If she keeps it, how will she support herself and the baby? Will the baby's father be involved in raising the child? Will her own parents be involved? If Cindy chooses to keep her baby, her having to make choices will never stop. For many years to come she will have to make many decisions that will help her child grow to adulthood.

Should pregnant teenagers have to make choices when it comes to giving birth? Some adults believe that a pregnant teen should not be allowed to decide what to do about her pregnancy, that her parents or the law should tell her what to do and how to behave. But freedom of choice about how to lead one's life is a right that belongs to all Americans. And yet it is also a right we must earn every day. Any teenager who believes that he or she has the right to choose sex also has a duty to know what that choice means. A young female needs to understand how her choice will affect others, including her parents, her boyfriend, the child she may have, and society, which may have to support her and her child.

The Choice To Have Sex

For many girls like Cindy, sex doesn't seem like something they choose. It seems more like something that happens to them before they realize it. Of course every girl does have a choice, but physical things that happen in her body when she becomes sexually excited can make it difficult for her to keep a clear head. This is usually true for the young man as well.

So it is important that a young woman make her choice *before* she gets into a situation that will make it difficult if not impossible for her to choose wisely. She should ask herself if she really feels ready for sex, and its possible results.

Every female has to make her own choice in the end, but she should also consider the people she loves and what they might want her to do. What are her moral values? How important are they? How important are they to her parents? Is she willing to risk hurting people she loves and possibly disrupting their lives by not taking responsibility for her actions?

If possible, she should try to talk to her parents about sex. For most young people that isn't easy, but it usually proves to be helpful. If she can't talk to her parents, she should try another adult with whom she can talk openly: an older sister or brother, a friend or relative, teacher or school counselor, pastor, priest or rabbi. She might feel embarrassed at first, or worried about what they will think. But if she isn't mature enough to talk about sex with people who can give helpful advice, then she probably isn't mature enough for a sexual relationship.

If a concerned teenager decides she isn't ready for sex, she needs to avoid getting into situations where she isn't fully in control of her feelings. She should make sure her boyfriend understands how she feels. She should not let him pressure her. He may have reasons that sound very convincing, but no reason is good enough to make a young woman do something she doesn't feel she should do.

What It Means To Choose Sex

Sooner or later young people decide that the time is right to try having sex. Whatever their age, teenagers must understand what that choice means.

For a young woman, it means two serious physical risks: catching a disease, and getting pregnant. A number of diseases can be transmitted only by sexual contact, the most serious of which is

AIDS. AIDS has no cure; it always leads to death. There are other dangerous diseases that can also be caught through sexual contact (just one is herpes simplex, which infects you for the rest of your life). Anyone who is sexually active needs to know about such diseases and how to protect herself/himself from them. Information can be obtained from health clinics, family planning centers, your school nurse or the library.

Then there's the risk of pregnancy. A girl who chooses sex must ask herself if she is ready to have a baby. If not, then she needs to practice birth control. Even then, birth control methods are not guaranteed.

There are many false notions about pregnancy. For example: a girl can't get pregnant the first time she has sex, or she can't get pregnant until she reaches a certain age. How about this one: douching after intercourse will prevent pregnancy. These and many other notions are incorrect. The truth is that as soon as she begins experiencing menstruation, no matter how young, a female can get pregnant. In fact, she becomes fertile about four weeks before her first period, so she can actually get pregnant before she has ever had a period. That's why birth control is a must to avoid pregnancy.

The simplest way to find out about birth control is to see a doctor or health care professional. Most birth control methods are only available from a doctor, who will be able to give advice about their proper use. A girl who would rather not talk to her family doctor can go to a clinic or a family planning center such as Planned Parenthood. (Don't be confused by the term "family planning": places like Planned Parenthood also help people plan to *not* become parents until they are ready.) Most clinics keep a young woman's choice of birth control completely private.

A teenager who doesn't know where to go for birth control information, or is worried about

These are contraceptives—methods for preventing pregnancy. They include a foam with applicator, three types of intrauterine devices, a diaphragm, birth control pills and condoms. The pill is still the most popular and effective method to prevent pregnancy.

the cost, can contact her city or county health department for help in finding a clinic she can trust. A school nurse can also provide useful information.

Condoms

The only effective type of birth control one can get without seeing a doctor is the condom, or "rubber." But even those who choose this method should talk to a doctor about the proper way to use condoms. It's easy to get careless, and one mistake is all it takes. The condom looks a bit like a flimsy balloon and is worn by the male during intercourse. It works best when the woman uses a spermacidal (sperm-killing) foam at the same time. Both condoms and foam can be bought at most drugstores. When the condom and foam are used together properly, they are up to 98 percent effective, which means they will fail two times out of 100. But statistics also show that condoms fail far more often when used by teens. That's why it's so important to learn the right way to use them. Condoms have the added value of protecting both sexual partners from diseases. For this reason alone, a girl should always insist that her partner wear a condom, no matter what other kind of birth control she may also be using.

The condom is the only effective form of birth control available to males. All others must be used by the female. Birth control pills are taken by millions of women in the United States, but they can only be obtained with a doctor's prescription. No one should ever try to use someone else's birth control pills, diaphragm, or anything else that has been prescribed by a doctor. There are many different kinds of birth control pills, and different brands can affect a woman's body in different ways. A doctor will decide what kind of pill (or other birth control) is best for each individual, and will make sure she knows how to use it properly. Birth control pills must be taken every day. Even one missed day makes this method unreliable. Also, the pill won't work well until it has been taken for 30 days. When used properly, birth control pills are up to 99 percent effective, which is better than any other form of birth control.

The pill, however, can increase the risk of certain health problems in some women. Two other forms of birth control—the diaphragm and IUD—are almost as effective (about 97 or 98 percent) and may be a better choice, especially for some younger women. The diaphragm is a specially fitted rubber cup (used with spermacidal cream or jelly) which is inserted just before having sex. The IUD is a small plastic or metal coil that is inserted by a doctor into the woman's uterus. It can be left in place for as long as two or three years, with an occasional check-up. Both these methods are fairly trouble-free but, like all birth control methods, they must be used with care to be safe and effective.

No other methods of birth control are dependable. The rhythm method involves having sex only at certain times of the month during which the woman is not fertile. But it's impossible for a woman to know for sure when she is fertile, and many women—especially young women—don't have menstrual cycles that are regular enough to make this method trustworthy. Even less safe is the withdrawal method, in which the man avoids ejaculating inside the woman's body. This method results in pregnancy for three out of ten couples who use it.

Some teenagers think there are other ways to avoid becoming pregnant, such as using plastic wrap in place of a condom, or using certain positions during intercourse. None of these work. Aside from not having sex at all, the only effective and accepted ways to prevent a pregnancy are those few discussed above. No means of birth control is 100 percent effective, but if a female follows a doctor's advice about birth control, she can greatly reduce her chances of becoming pregnant.

For a lot of teenagers, birth control seems like a hassle and totally unromantic. A young woman may also be embarrassed to ask a doctor or a nurse or a pharmacist about birth control. But she should never let such reservations stop her from making a choice that could keep her life on track. The inconvenience of birth control is small compared to the inconvenience of pregnancy and childbirth. The people she can turn to for birth control want to help her. It's their job.

The least effective method of birth control is the one so many teenagers count on: dumb luck. But even if her luck holds for a while, every time a girl has sex her odds get worse. She will pay a high price when her "luck" eventually runs out. The worst mistake she can make is to think, "It can't happen to me."

Choosing Pregnancy

Nearly one out of every four teenage mothers admits that she got pregnant on purpose. For some young girls, having a baby seems like a good way to be grownup. These girls are tired of being treated like children and want to prove that they are really women by having a child of their own. For some, having a baby seems exciting, or it may be a way to get attention, to feel special.

Some girls like the idea of having a cute little baby around to love and cuddle, or they see something romantic in the idea of having a baby. It may seem like a completion of her love for the young man in her life, or a way to force her boyfriend to stay and take her seriously.

Having a baby may also be a way to get back at someone: like her parents, or the world. It's an act of rebellion, or a declaration of independence, a way of saying "you're not my boss because you can't stop me from doing this."

For others, especially young women living in inner city areas where crime and poverty are severe problems, having a baby can seem like an escape, a fast way out of a troubled home life. Or they believe having a baby will create a love that has been missing from their lives.

Any girl who believes that getting pregnant might be a good idea for any reason should think carefully about how good her reason is. Getting pregnant takes only a few minutes or less, but carrying a baby takes nine months. And raising a child will take over her life for many years, with no time off for good behavior.

Is someone who is considering pregnancy ready to give up youth and freedom and face grown-up responsibilities? Having a baby can be a way to escape problems, but new problems that come with taking care of a helpless baby can make her old problems seem tiny. A baby can be lovable and cuddly some of the time, but what about when he or she is sick, or hungry and crying? What if the young mother has no one to help her and she gets sick herself?

A girl who thinks she'd like to be a mother should also know that pregnancy is more dangerous for a teenager. She is twice as likely to die in childbirth than an older woman. Children born to teenage mothers have a higher risk of having birth defects or health problems. And the child of a very young mother is twice as likely to die before reaching his or her first birthday.

On the economic side, a girl who has a baby while still in school often has to cut short her education. Young single mothers find it hard to support themselves and their children without at least a high school diploma.

Marriages between teenage parents usually end in divorce. Taking care of a baby when a couple is young creates great stress. The young couple begins to feel trapped, and may take it out on each other or on the baby.

Women who start families while still in their teens often live in poverty the rest of their lives. Their children will probably also live in poverty, and have fewer opportunities as they grow up. The odds of their having a better life are not good.

So the choice to raise a baby while still a teenager can be very costly, not only for the mother and father, but also for the child.

When is a woman old enough to have a child? Some people may never be mature enough to face the responsibilities of parenting; others might be ready at a very young age. One thing seems clear: no one is really ready to have a child until she can support it and still pursue the things in life she wants for herself.

III. Pregnant

If a young woman gets pregnant unexpectedly, she has some difficult choices ahead of her.

A girl who suspects she is pregnant needs to be tested as soon as possible. The longer she waits, the fewer choices she will have regarding her pregnancy. Also, a developing embryo is at risk without early medical attention.

Some early symptoms of pregnancy can appear within the first two or three weeks after conception. These include: nausea or "morning sickness," so called because it often occurs in the morning; having to go to the bathroom more often than usual; swelling of breasts or ankles; mood changes; and fatigue. But the clearest warning sign is a missed period. If a woman's period is more

Birthing classes are helpful not only for the information they provide pregnant teenagers but for the social benefit of being with others that share your concerns.

than two weeks late and she has had sex within the past 45 days, she could very well be pregnant.

Some young women ignore the warning signs. They don't want to believe they are pregnant, so they think of other explanations such as, "I must have the flu." Or "My period isn't late, it was just very light this month." Ignoring signs of pregnancy will only lead to more problems later, so it's good to be tested as soon as possible.

Home pregnancy tests are sold in drug stores, but the instructions can be confusing and must be followed carefully. Even then, the tests aren't always right. If a home pregnancy test shows positive, a woman should make an appointment right away to be tested by a doctor. If the home test shows negative, she should have herself checked by a doctor if she still doesn't get her period.

Going to a doctor or clinic early in pregnancy is important. Not only will a girl find out for sure whether or not she is pregnant, but she will have help at once if she is. No matter what she decides to do about her pregnancy, she will need a doctor's care.

Some clinics have special services for young people, or they may be able to recommend another clinic that does. When a girl first calls, they will want to know about her symptoms and how late her period is. They can tell her about the cost of the test and what she should bring with her (usually a urine sample). Some clinics offer free pregnancy tests; others charge according to how much a woman can afford; and some charge a flat rate.

At the clinic, the doctor will normally do a urine test to find out whether or not the woman is pregnant. In certain cases, a blood test may also be given. The result of a urine test is usually known the same day. A blood test takes a day or two longer.

When a test comes up positive, the doctor will usually recommend a pelvic examination to find out how far along the pregnancy is and to make sure the mother is in good physical condition. A girl's first pelvic exam may make her nervous and uncomfortable, but she will soon learn that it's part of every healthy woman's life, even when she isn't pregnant.

Getting Help

A teenager is usually shocked when she finds out she is pregnant. She may feel bad about herself for getting into such a mess, but she needs to find a way to forgive herself and get help. Everyone makes mistakes, but now's the time to start making some right choices to find assistance. Above all, she shouldn't be afraid or too proud to ask for help. No one should have to face an unwanted pregnancy alone.

It's important for a pregnant teenager to remember that she isn't alone; she won't shock a doctor with her problem. Remember, over a million teenagers get pregnant each year. She may not find much comfort in that, but it means many professional people are out there to help her. They won't treat her like a freak or a monster. The worst thing she can do is to try to avoid her problem by pretending it doesn't exist.

Sooner or later her parents will have to know, unless she can get an abortion without their consent. She may want to talk to them before she talks to anyone else, or she might find it easier to start with someone else she can trust.

If she's worried that her parents will try to make her do something she doesn't want to do, then she should get as much information as she can before she tells them. She needs to know all her options so she can make the decision that is best for her. No matter how loving and supportive parents may be, they often find it hard to accept that they no longer have the power to make their daughter's choices for her. They can only advise

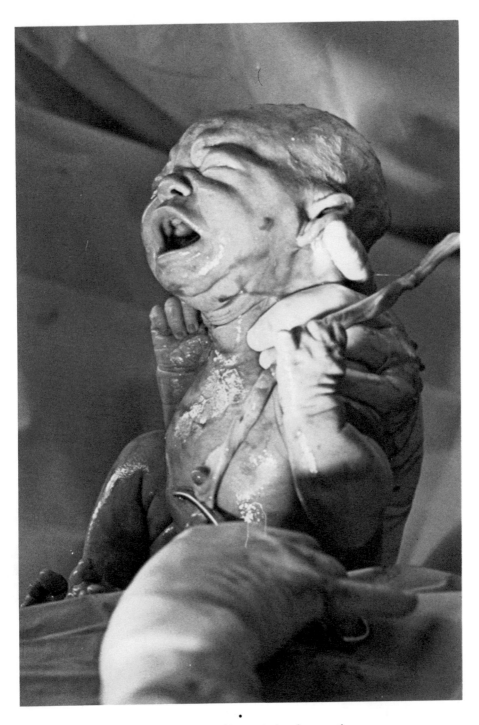

This is the moment unlike any other for a mother—
the birth of her child.

her to do what they feel is best. She must make her own choice.

A girl who has no one else to talk to can go to Planned Parenthood or another family-planning clinic. In most cases, these clinics will give important information about her options without trying to influence her decision. If she feels that she is being pushed in one direction, she should go somewhere else.

Talking her problem over with people she trusts will help a pregnant teenager feel she's in control of her life. That's important, because she will need to see things clearly in order to decide what to do next.

Early in a pregnancy, a woman has three options:

1. Having an abortion to end the pregnancy before the fetus has grown enough to live outside the mother's body.

2. Giving birth and raising the baby herself.

3. Relinquishing the baby (or "giving it up") for adoption.

The following chapters will look at these three options and what they mean.

IV. Abortion

At the present time, about two out of every five pregnant teenage girls in the United States choose to have abortions. The issue of abortion is one of the most controversial in our nation. Is abortion immoral? Does abortion kill a human life or does it only prevent a human life from coming into being? Should a woman have control over her own body, even if it means stopping a new life from developing? Should the government forbid abortion or restrict it in any way? Should minors have the same abortion rights as adults? Should the government help pay for abortions for women who want but can't afford them?

This short book cannot begin to address these questions, however, most teenagers have a sense of their own beliefs about abortion. But when a girl actually becomes pregnant, she may find herself wanting to re-examine her beliefs.

Abortion is legal throughout the United States, but each state makes its own laws about how, when and where an abortion can be obtained. Most states will not provide public money to pay for abortions.

Some states will not allow a minor to have an abortion without parental consent. A girl who feels that she can't talk to her parents about being pregnant or having an abortion, or whose parents refuse to give permission, may be able to seek special permission from a judge. People who work in state-licensed abortion clinics should know about the options allowed by their state.

Whether she talks to her parents or not, a young woman thinking about having an abortion will want to get some professional advice. She should seek more than one point of view. For example, if one person tells her that abortion is wrong, that it's a sin or murder, then she should try to find someone else who feels differently and can say why. She shouldn't let anyone tell her what to do. Even if her own parents insist on one choice or another, she should make sure it's a choice she believes in.

She may also want to talk to her sexual partner who shares responsibility for her pregnancy. He might be able to offer emotional support and advice. Or he might also be able to help pay for an abortion, if that is her choice. Again, he can't tell her what to do about her pregnancy, but since he helped create her pregnancy, there's nothing wrong with asking him to help decide what to do about it.

As soon as she is sure abortion is the right choice for her, a woman must take action. The longer she waits to have an abortion, the more difficult, dangerous and expensive it will be. After a certain point, abortion will cease to be an option at all.

Making Plans For An Abortion

The safest abortions are those done in the first three months of pregnancy (also called the first *trimester*). In many states a woman can get an abortion in the second trimester (months four through six of pregnancy), but this may involve a riskier, more expensive method. With very few exceptions, an abortion after six months is not possible.

The first step is to find out where to go for a safe abortion. Clinics that give pregnancy tests can sometimes do abortions. If not, they will recommend a place.

A woman should be sure to find a clean, safe, professional clinic which has been licensed by the state to perform abortions. The doctors should be specialists in obstetrics and gynecology, often called "ob-gyn" doctors, who specialize in childbirth and women's health. A good clinic will offer counseling services and be set up for an emergency should something go wrong during an abortion. Abortions—particularly in the first trimester—are very safe, safer than giving birth. Only on rare occasions do complications occur.

In most cases, a first-trimester abortion will

cost $200 or $300. Some states offer financial assis-tance to women who can't pay for an abortion on their own, but most do not. A girl who can't afford the cost will have to get financial assistance. If her parents can't provide the money, maybe the young man who helped create the pregnancy will help pay for an abortion. Maybe friends can lend her the money, or if she has a job, she might ask for a salary advance. If all else fails, she can talk to the people at her clinic—or try another clinic—and explain her problem.

However expensive an abortion may seem, having a child is even more expensive. Lack of money should never make the decision for a preg-nant teenager. No matter how desperate, any female should never have to resort to an illegal,

•
Many young women choose to end an unplanned pregnancy through abortion, a legal medical procedure that continues to generate controversy in the courts, state legislatures and in public protests such as these.
•

unsafe abortion by someone who isn't licensed to perform the procedure.

There are many myths about ways to end a pregnancy by yourself like beating your stomach, falling down stairs, eating or drinking something, or inserting something sharp into your cervix (the opening of the uterus). Never try any of these do-it-yourself methods. They don't work, and they can be very dangerous. They can also cause serious injury, illness, severe infection, or even death. The only safe choice for an abortion is to raise the money and find a licensed professional.

The Abortion Procedure

A first-trimester abortion can be done in a few hours and requires no hospital stay. Several things happen before the abortion itself. A patient is asked questions about her pregnancy and medical history. The clinic asks about any serious diseases or operations she has had, and whether she is currently taking any medication or has allergies to certain drugs such as penicillin. Urine and blood tests and a pelvic exam are given.

The usual procedure takes about 10 to 20 minutes. The patient is given a mild drug to relax her and a local anesthetic (pain-killer) to numb the cervix. Sometimes an abortion is done under general anesthetic, which means putting the patient to sleep for the entire procedure. In the most common procedure, a tube is then inserted into the cervix and the tissue of the embryo is removed by suction. There may be some pain, but it shouldn't last long or be too severe.

After the procedure is finished, the patient is given time to recover. The doctor will examine the tissue that has been removed to make certain the abortion is completed. Then the patient is told how to take care of herself in the following few weeks and when to return for a follow-up exam. This follow-up is important, even if there may be no obvious problems. Most women recover very quickly. They may experience some light bleeding—similar to menstrual bleeding—for several days, and they may also have mild cramps for a few days.

Abortions after the first trimester involve a longer stay, more than one visit or, in some cases, a day or two in the hospital. Abortions after about the sixteenth week of pregnancy require riskier methods and the chance of complications is greater.

A woman who makes the choice to have an abortion and feels strongly that it's the right choice for her will probably not suffer any serious emotional effects afterward. Most women say they feel relieved. Crying and feeling depressed for a short while after an abortion are normal reactions, and most women will find it helpful to talk to someone about their feelings.

Someone who has been pushed into having an abortion, however, or who was never completely sure that was what she really wanted to do, may have a rougher time getting over it. The clinic may have a counselor or be able to recommend someone who can help her deal with her feelings.

A safe, legal abortion will not affect a woman's ability to get pregnant again in the future. However, repeated abortions can complicate a future pregnancy and make it harder to carry a child all the way to a natural birth. That's why abortion should never be thought of as a practical form of birth control, but rather as a last resort to end an unwanted pregnancy.

Abortion isn't the right choice for everyone. Some women have religious or moral objections, while some simply have a strong emotional reaction against aborting their own pregnancies. Options for those who decide against abortion are discussed later. In the next chapter is important information about care for those who choose to carry their pregnancies to full term.

V. Nine Months Of Pregnancy

TEEN MOTHERS

Health care for a pregnant woman is called *prenatal* (before birth) care, and is extremely important. Regular visits to a doctor insure that the baby is developing normally and that proper care is being taken by the mother.

Studies show that pregnant teenagers have a higher risk of health problems related to pregnancy than older women. Their developing babies are also at higher risk, not only for birth defects but for premature birth or low birth weight. This can mean health problems for the rest of the child's life. The only reason health problems are more common for pregnant teenagers and their babies is that teenagers are less likely to get proper prenatal care.

Prenatal care should begin as early as possi-

•

These 17-year-old girls attend a special school in Colorado for teen mothers so that their education will not be interrupted just because they have chosen to keep their babies. The school has a nursery and other special facilities.

•

ble in the pregnancy. Much of a baby's most important development happens in the first three months, and how a mother takes care of herself can have a profound effect on that development. She should definitely see a doctor no later than the end of her twelfth week of pregnancy.

Prenatal care is available at just about any hospital or health clinic or from a private doctor. Like any medical care, prenatal care can be expensive. A county health department or any doctor or hospital can recommend a low-cost clinic to women who can't afford the expense. Any pregnant woman under the age of 21 can apply for financial help from Medicaid. She may also be able to get assistance from the government's Aid to Families with Dependent Children (AFDC) program.

On her first visit for prenatal care, a woman is asked about her medical history. She is given blood and urine tests to check for certain diseases or disorders. Then she has a thorough physical to make sure she is in good health for her pregnancy. This includes a pelvic exam to check for any problems in her reproductive system. The doctor will also give her very important information about home care during pregnancy.

Home Care

Good nutrition is vital to a baby's development. The baby is being fed by the mother's body, so she must make sure to feed herself well. Milk and other dairy products such as yogurt, cheese and ice cream are important. So is plenty of protein in the form of meat, fish, poultry, eggs, beans and nuts. Vegetables and fruit on a daily basis provide necessary vitamins. The carbohydrates in bread and cereals are also important. A pregnant woman's doctor may advise her to take vitamins. If so, she should take only the kind and amount recommended. Too many vitamins, or the wrong kind, can do more harm than good.

A pregnant woman has to be very careful about what she puts into her body. Everything she eats, drinks, injects or breathes will find its way into her baby. There are many substances to avoid; one of the worst is alcohol. Even one drink of beer, wine or hard alcohol taken by a pregnant woman can affect her baby's development. The more she drinks the higher the risk that her baby will be born with severe birth defects. Alcoholic drinks now carry warnings to pregnant women on their labels.

Caffeine, found in coffee, some kinds of tea, and colas should also be avoided. Also risky are diet soft drinks and any diet foods containing chemical sweeteners like saccharin or aspartame.

A woman who smokes should do everything she can to quit during pregnancy, as nicotine is a dangerous poison for a developing baby. A mother should also avoid exposure to any diseases, such as chicken pox and rubella (German measles).

Finally, a mother must avoid all drugs, both illegal (like marijuana, speed, heroin, cocaine or crack) and legal—even the kinds that don't require a prescription. She should always make sure a doctor knows she is pregnant before she accepts prescriptions for any drug. Even household medicines such as aspirin, cold medicine or a stomach treatment should have a doctor's approval.

Problems in pregnancy may be accompanied by warning signs such as unusual bleeding, swelling, pain, blurred vision, continuous vomiting, a headache, or fever that won't go away. A pregnant woman who experiences any such worrisome symptoms should call her doctor immediately.

Life During Pregnancy

A pregnant woman experiences great physical and emotional changes. Her hormones are on "overdrive," which can make her very moody. She may find herself swinging unpredictably between very high and very low moods. She may cry or become short-tempered for no obvious reason. She may become unusually happy or optimistic. She may also withdraw into daydreams.

Many of these emotional changes are directly tied to the hormonal changes in her body. During the early months of pregnancy she will probably experience occasional nausea and unpredictable appetites and cravings. Her breasts may become larger and more tender. She may feel tired all the time.

Later in her pregnancy she may begin to have cramps, backaches and general discomfort. She may have trouble sleeping even though she feels tired. The size of her belly may make it difficult to feel comfortable in any position. By the ninth month she may feel shortness of breath and occasional indigestion. Sometime in the last few weeks the baby will "drop," moving head down and lower onto her hips to prepare for birth. This usually happens 10 to 14 days before birth.

As her body changes she might begin to feel self-conscious in public, especially if she looks very young and noticeably pregnant. People may say insensitive things to her. She'll be able to keep her spirits up if she reminds herself that she is doing everything she can to take responsibility for her life and the new life growing inside her.

A pregnant teenager should look for opportunities to talk to women who have had babies. Her own mother can probably be a great source of information, advice and emotional support. If not, she should find other helpful women who understand what she is going through and how to make it easier.

The teenager who finds living at home during pregnancy too stressful does have other options. If she can't afford her own place, she may be able to move in with a relative or adult friend. She can also try to find a group maternity home where she will live with other unmarried, pregnant young women. She will be given guidance and care to help get through her pregnancy with fewer problems. In some maternity homes, a girl can even stay for some time after her baby's birth.

A very good idea for all pregnant women is to take childbirth classes. Such classes are often offered in clinics or hospitals that provide prenatal care. Most local Red Cross or Y.W.C.A centers also offer classes and other services for pregnant teenagers.

If at all possible, a teen mother should try to continue school during pregnancy. Some schools have special programs for pregnant students so they can continue their regular education while learning about pregnancy, childbirth and parenting. Even schools that offer no special programs must allow a pregnant girl to go to class if she chooses to do so.

VI. Adoption

Some girls can't imagine having to raise a baby by themselves, or they know it would be too great a burden for them and their families. A young woman in that situation may want to consider putting her baby up for adoption so that it can be raised by a couple who will be better able to provide a good home.

Putting a baby up for adoption is a hard choice to make. It means giving up a child who has literally been a part of you for nine months. But sometimes it can be the most loving, unselfish gift a woman can give her baby: a chance at a better life. She gives herself that chance, too, by putting herself in a better position to pursue her education, find a good job, and become a responsible adult. She can have another baby later if she wants, and be able to offer it the kind of life it deserves.

A young woman considering adoption for her baby should talk with a counselor about what it involves and how to proceed. She can get counseling at any adoption agency, or her state or county may have an adoption program that can put her in touch with a counselor. Her doctor or clinic may also be able to provide information.

Those considering adoption should begin making plans as soon as possible. The process can take some time, and later in her pregnancy a woman will have other things to think about. Waiting to explore adoption until after the baby's birth will only make things more difficult.

Adoptions can be arranged through an adoption agency or by what is called private or independent adoption. An adoption agency will take care of all the arrangements for the mother. In a private adoption, the mother makes more of the arrangements herself with the help of a lawyer. Although private adoptions can have advantages, a very young mother is usually better off going through an adoption agency. Both choices are discussed below.

Adoption Agencies

Some adoption agencies are run by churches or other private organizations, and some are not. Some have been set up by groups strongly opposed to abortion. If this matters to the pregnant woman, she may want to ask about an agency's relationship to other groups right away. This is most important if she has not yet made up her mind to choose adoption. If an agency is opposed to abortion, they may try very hard to influence a woman away from that choice.

In adoption through an agency, a mother turns her baby over to the agency, who then places the child with carefully chosen parents. The birthmother may or may not be allowed to meet the new parents, but she will usually have some say in the choice. For example, she can tell the agency what kind of family she wants her baby to go to, and the agency will do its best to make a good match. Or she may be given a choice of several families so she can choose the one she feels will be best for her baby. She can always ask questions about the people who want to adopt her baby.

Couples who wish to adopt a child (called "adoptive parents") have already been screened carefully by the agency. The agency makes sure that adoptive parents will provide a good home, love the baby, and be able to raise it well.

There are many advantages to arranging adoption through an agency. Agencies provide counseling for the birthmother and help see that she receives proper health care while pregnant. They can also help her find financial assistance or a maternity home, if needed. They will find adoptive parents with the right qualities to raise a child, and will take care of all legal matters related to adoption.

Private Adoption

Private adoption is legal in most states, but the exact laws controlling this kind of adoption are

different from state to state. In most cases, private adoption means turning the baby over to someone already known to the birthmother. She has complete control over who will take her baby, as she chooses the new parents herself. In an agency adoption she may never know who the adoptive parents are.

In a private adoption, no matter who the adoptive parents may be—even if they are related to the mother—she will need the help of a lawyer. For an adoption to be legal, certain procedures must be followed; certain papers must be signed and filed with the state. Lawyers who specialize in private adoption can be found in the phone book under "Adoption." These lawyers can sometimes suggest possible adoptive parents, if the mother hasn't found any herself. To make sure that some-one is watching out for the birthmother's interests, she should always have her own lawyer rather than share the same lawyer with the adoptive parents.

One disadvantage to private adoption is that the adoptive parents are not investigated until after the baby is in their care. Remember that an adop-

•

These parents are adopting their second child. Teenage mothers who cannot afford to raise their own baby can provide a good home for the child through adoption.

•

tion agency always investigates possible parents before the baby is turned over.

A pregnant woman should beware of any privately arranged adoption in which she is offered more money than what her expenses will be. Some people are so desperate for a child that they will offer large sums of money to the birthmother. But such "baby selling" is illegal in every state.

Open Adoption

Until recently, almost all adoptions arranged in the United States were "closed" adoptions. The birthmother was never told who the adoptive parents were or where they lived, and the child and his or her adoptive parents were never told who the natural mother was. This was thought to be best for everyone involved. In order to protect everyone's privacy, the state sealed all the papers relating to the adoption, and no one was ever allowed to see them.

In recent years, however, "open" adoption has become a choice favored by some social workers and adoption agencies. In an open adoption, the birthmother meets the adoptive parents, and they may choose to stay in contact as the child grows up.

Now, even in a closed adoption, the birthmother may be given the choice of signing a release form so that her child, once he or she has grown up, can choose to contact her. But even if a release is signed, the mother can change her mind at any future time if she decides she would rather not be contacted by her child. Whether she goes with an independent or an agency adoption, a birthmother should be sure she understands what her rights will be regarding future contact with her child. If using an agency, she should find out what their policy is regarding open adoption.

Relinquishing The Baby

The adoption of a baby doesn't become

legal and permanent until the birthmother signs *relinquishment* papers (relinquishment means giving the baby up), and by law these papers can't be signed until she has left the hospital after the baby's birth. This means that she can change her mind at any time until she has signed this final agreement regardless of what other papers she may have signed. It doesn't matter what promises she has made to anyone, or if the adoptive parents have paid her expenses. But once she and the baby's father have signed the relinquishment papers, she can no longer change her mind.

Most of the decisions about pregnancy belong to the mother alone, but most states require that the decision to give a child up for adoption be shared by the baby's natural father, or at least that he be informed. A mother may be required by law to make an honest effort to obtain his consent and have him sign the relinquishment papers. If she fails to do so, the baby's life could be disrupted at some point in the future.

In most cases the birthmother will be given a chance to see her baby before it is given to the adoptive parents, but the mother can always choose not to see the child.

How will a young mother feel about giving up her baby? If she has had good adoption counseling, she has been able to prepare for the emotions she will likely experience. But no matter how well prepared she is, she will almost surely find it very hard when the time comes. Giving up a baby to adoption is in some ways like experiencing the death of a loved one. A period of mourning is perfectly natural. But the pain she feels at giving her baby a good home doesn't mean she has made a mistake. Instead that pain represents a sacrifice she has made for the welfare of her baby. She can be proud that she had the strength to do what was best for her child.

VII. Parenthood

Of those pregnant teen-agers who decide to have their babies, most will go on to raise the baby themselves rather than put it up for adoption. For many girls this seems like the easiest or least selfish choice, or the one that they think other people expect. They may think, "I made the mistake, now I have to live with it."

But a teen mother's decision to raise a child will have far-reaching consequences for both her child and herself. She should remember how she saw her future before she got pregnant. What were her priorities? Did she plan to finish school and maybe go to college? When did she think she might get married? Did she hope to travel before settling down? All of these plans will probably have to change if she decides to raise the baby herself. A young pregnant female should choose this option only if she feels that it is the best choice for her, her family, and especially for her child. If these are not her reasons, she should re-evaluate her decision.

One of the worst reasons to become a teenage parent is to avoid facing any other option and not make a decision about them. Another bad reason is to try to make other people happy. Perhaps a pregnant teen's parents are urging her to keep the baby, and they may even promise to help with money and child care. The baby's father may want her to keep the child. Or maybe her friends are telling her that giving up a child isn't natural. It doesn't matter who is trying to influence her, it is her choice. Everyone else—parents, boyfriend, girlfriends—can change their minds once the baby is born. The mother can't.

A number of other things must also be con-sidered. Will she raise the child as a single parent, or is marriage an option? If she can't or doesn't wish to get married, what will be her "support sys-tem"—not just her source of money to live on, but also her source of emotional support and child-care assistance? No matter how mature and self-supporting she may be, it isn't realistic to think that she will be able to raise a child completely on her own.

Marriage

A young woman should never feel pressured to get married just because she is pregnant. Regardless of how she feels about getting married, she also needs to think about the young man. Is he really ready to commit to her for life? Would he have been ready to do that even before she got pregnant? If he is in school, is he ready to drop out and get a job to help support the baby? What kind of a job will he be able to get and how much will it pay? Is he mature enough to face this kind of responsibility without feeling resentful?

These are hard questions, but they must be answered honestly. Most teenage marriages that result from an unplanned pregnancy don't work out. There are too many pressures on a young couple and these pressures only become harder with a baby to raise.

Even for those lucky ones who manage to make this kind of marriage work, the price can be very high. If the parents have to leave school, chances are they will only be able to get low-paying jobs. Supporting a family is expensive. They may never be able to go back to school or to get job training.

The situation may be different if they can count on the support of their families. With grandparents helping to take care of the baby, the young parents may be able to stay in school. With financial support from their families, some of the pressure is taken off a young couple.

The worst thing a teen mother can do is rush into a marriage "for the baby's sake." A child rarely benefits from an unhappy or loveless marriage. The father can still be part of the baby's life

The romance of an engagement ring, and an impending marriage, are not automatic
when a teenage girl becomes pregnant. Many teens who choose to keep their
babies must raise them alone, and marriages arranged because of an unplanned
pregnancy often end in divorce.

even if they don't choose to get married. He can visit and help with child care as much as he and the mother want. She doesn't have to marry him for him to be a part of her child's life.

If Marriage Isn't An Option

A baby needs constant care and attention. A mother who can't or doesn't wish to get married must be prepared to give that care and attention by herself, or arrange to get help.

One of the best sources of help may be her own family, but she shouldn't assume that her parents or others in the family will always be willing and able to help. If she continues to live with her parents, she needs to know what they will expect of her. Will her responsibilities to the home and family be the same as they always were, or will her parents expect more, or less?

She should also make sure she and her parents reach an understanding about who is in charge when it comes to raising the baby. As the baby's mother, she may feel that she should have control over how he or she is raised. But if she relies on her family for a place to live, money and child care, they may expect to have something to say about the baby too. A compromise may be necessary.

On Her Own

If a young mother can't count on her family for support, she needs to start making other plans as soon as possible before the baby is born. Some communities have full-service programs for pregnant women that will provide for health care, living arrangements, and even child care to allow the mother to continue her education or go to work. If there is no such program, she will have to do the planning and providing herself.

First, where will she live and how will she pay her way? She may be able to stay in a home for unwed mothers for a while, but eventually she will have to find her own place. She can look into sharing a place with another young single mother. Living with someone else can be difficult, but it can also have advantages. Two mothers can share the burden of child care, and such an arrangement might ease the loneliness that young mothers often feel when they're on their own.

As for money, a young single mother can look for help from a number of sources, including the father of the child. He is required by law to provide money for child support, whether or not he and the mother are married. But if he is still in school or working at a low-paying job, he probably won't be able to contribute much.

Most single teenage mothers receive money from various government programs, including direct welfare payments, food stamps, and child-care assistance. She may also be able to take a part-time job and earn some additional money without having to give up any of the welfare money.

A young mother on her own will discover that money isn't her only problem. She will need child-care help. Even if she doesn't plan to go back to school or get a job, she will need to arrange to have some time to herself, to just rest and relieve some of the tension that builds up from taking care of a baby.

In the beginning, friends and family will probably be eager to help out. But once the novelty of the baby wears off, the young mother may find she has no reliable child-care support. One solution is to find good babysitters, people she knows she can trust. Good babysitters are hard to find, however, and they cost money. The same is true of good day-care centers. A day-care center should be safe, clean and have enough staff to look after all the children in its care. Some communities offer free or low-cost day care while a mother is in school or a job-training program.

All teenagers who choose to carry their baby to term should have prenatal counseling to learn everything they can, not only about the birth process, but what comes after.

A young mother looking for a job should also know that some large companies now offer day-care services for their workers. City or county employment offices may have information on such companies.

Another necessity for a mother and her baby is health care. If she can't afford a health plan, she should look into free or low-cost clinics in her area by calling her county's children's services or health department.

No matter how old a mother is, the responsibility of raising a child on her own is huge. But if she takes it on with open eyes, plans ahead and builds a support system, she'll be in a much better position to provide for her baby's needs and her own well-being.

A New Beginning

As with any setback in life, a teenager has two ways to look at an unwanted pregnancy. She can consider it a hopeless disaster, and decide early on to have an abortion, or she can see it as a challenge and carry the baby to full term. That allows her to either keep the baby or give it up for adoption.

In either case, she should immediately get professional advice, take control of her life, and see that she does have choices. If she takes positive action at the start, she will have a much better chance of feeling she has done the right thing for herself. She will also have the best chance of avoiding another unplanned pregnancy.

The choice is hers.

For More Information

A teenager need not face any of her difficult choices about sex and pregnancy alone. She can obtain help and information from a variety of sources.

One of the best places to start is the phone book. It should have listings under "Birth Control" or "Health Services" that will include clinics for birth control, pregnancy tests or abortion services. There may also be listings under "abortion" and "adoption."

Government offices can also offer much help to a pregnant teenager. Phone numbers for city and county agencies are usually found in a special "Government" section of the phone book under the name of the city or county.

Most county health departments have special offices that offer information on clinics for birth control or abortions. Many also have an office for adoption services. A city or county department of children's services can usually refer a pregnant teenager to low-cost prenatal care or a maternity home. Children's service or social service departments can provide information about welfare assistance programs available to teenage mothers. A young woman who has trouble finding the right government department for her needs should simply call any general health services or social services phone number and ask for help.

Information about abortion laws and services across the country can be obtained from the **National Abortion Federation Hotline: 1-800-772-9100.**

Those who have decided on adoption can get information from **Birthright: 1-800-848-5683**. Women considering a call to Birthright should know that the group is actively opposed to abortion rights.

The Red Cross and Y.W.C.A. are also good sources for information and assistance, as is Planned Parenthood. These organizations often offer classes for pregnant women. They sometimes have special programs for pregnant teenagers, and may be able to refer teenagers to maternity homes.

Glossary

ABORTION. The medical procedure for terminating a pregnancy.

ADOPTIVE PARENTS. A single parent or couple that choose to adopt a baby.

AIDS. (Acquired Immune Deficiency Syndrome.) A sexually-transmitted disease that shuts down the body's natural immune system.

BIRTHMOTHER. A mother who relinquishes her baby to adoptive parents.

BIRTH CONTROL. Any number of methods used by both males and females for preventing conception during sexual intercourse.

CERVIX. The opening to the uterus.

CONDOM. A sheath, usually rubber, worn on the male penis as a method of birth control.

FIRST TRIMESTER. The first three months of a pregnancy.

PRENATAL CARE. The health care a pregnant woman must have to make sure she and her baby remain healthy during the pregnancy.

Bibliography

Arms, Suzanne. *To Love and Let Go.* Alfred A. Knopf, 1983

Bell, Ruth, et. al. *Changing Bodies, Changing Lives.* Random House, 1980

Bode, Janet. *Kids Having Kids: The Unwed Teenage Parent.* Franklin Watts, 1980

Dash, Leon. *When Children Want Children: The Urban Crisis of Teenage Childbearing.* William Morrow and Company, 1989

Hansen, Caryl. *Your Choice: A Young Woman's Guide to Making Decisions about Unmarried Pregnancy.* Avon, 1980

Lindsay, Jeanne Warren. *Parents, Pregnant Teens and the Adoption Option.* Morning Glory Press, 1989

Lindsay, Jeanne Warren. *Pregnant Too Soon: Adoption Is an Option.* EMC Publishing, 1980; Morning Glory Press, 1988

Mansnerus, Laura. "Private Adoptions Aided by Expanding Network." *New York Times,* October 5, 1989

McCoy, Kathy. "If You Think You're Pregnant." *Seventeen,* August 1988

McCuen, Gary E., ed. *Children Having Children: Global Perspectives on Teenage Pregnancy.* G.E.M. Publications, 1988

McGuire, Paula. *It Won't Happen to Me.* Delacorte Press, 1983

O'Brien, Bev. "Mom...I'm Pregnant." Tyndale House Publishers, 1982

Richards, Arelene Kramer and Irene Willis. *Under 18 and Pregnant.* Lothrop, Lee & Shepard Books, 1983

Rolin, David Oliver. "The Struggle to Curb Teenage Pregnancy." *Scholastic Update*, January 15, 1988: 10-11

"Teenaged Mothers—17 Years Later." *Children Today*, January-February 1988: 2-4

Witt, Reni L. and Jeannine Masterson Michael, M.S.W., C.S.W. *Mom, I'm Pregnant.* Stein and Day, 1982

Index

Picture Credits